MATT KENSETH

IN THE FAST LANE

David and Patricia Armentrout

Rourke

Publishing LLC
Vero Beach, Florida 32964

www.rourkepublishing.com

PHOTO CREDITS: Pg. 5 ©Autostock; all other photos ©Getty Images

Title page: *Matt Kenseth leads the pack in the #17 DeWalt Ford.*

Editor: Robert Stengard-Olliges

Cover design by Nicola Stratford

Library of Congress Cataloging-in-Publication Data

Armentrout, David, 1962-
  Matt Kenseth : in the fast lane / David and Patricia Armentrout.
     p. cm. -- (In the fast lane)
  Includes index.
  ISBN 1-60044-219-6
  1. Kenseth, Matt---Juvenile literature. 2. Automobile racing
drivers--United States--Biography--Juvenile literature. I. Armentrout,
Patricia, 1960- II. Title. III. Series.
  GV1032.K455 A76 2007
  796.72092 B 22
                          2006011013

Printed in the USA

CG/CG

Rourke Publishing

www.rourkepublishing.com – sales@rourkepublishing.com
Post Office Box 3328, Vero Beach, FL 32964
1-800-394-7055

TABLE OF CONTENTS

MATT KENSETH

    Stock car racing's greatest prize is the **NASCAR** Nextel Cup (formerly Winston Cup). Many talented drivers spend their careers chasing the **championship**, only to fall short of the sports ultimate goal.

    Matt Kenseth is not just a talented driver. He is one of NASCAR's elite competitors. He won the Winston Cup championship in just his fourth season as a full-time Cup driver.

Born: March 10, 1972
Organization: NASCAR
Car: Ford #17
Car owner: Mark Martin
Team: Roush Racing
Sponsor: Dewalt

Matt's team goes to work on the #17 Dewalt Ford.

A GREAT START

Racing is not an easy sport to get into. It is very expensive and takes a lot of time and effort. Not everyone understands the sacrifices that must be made to race cars for a living, so it helps to grow up in a family that knows the sport.

Matt definitely had the support of his family. His father introduced him to racing. His father even bought Matt his first racecar. Matt didn't waste the opportunity. He scored his first victory at age 16, his first year racing.

FAST FACTS

Matt's first racecar was a 1981 Chevy Camaro.

Strapped in and ready for a practice run.

Matt drives the #17 Visine car in a Busch series race.

Matt paid his dues racing in local, state, and regional events near his family's home in Wisconsin. But Matt never lingered too long on his way to NASCAR. He learned what he could at each level and then moved on to the next.

Matt raced against many great competitors early in his career. A rival, Robbie Reiser, was so impressed with Matt that he would later give him his first chance to drive in NASCAR's Busch series.

NASCAR'S BUSCH SERIES

Robbie Reiser and Matt teamed up in 1997 to make their mark in NASCAR's Busch series. Robbie provided the team and Matt drove the car. In just 21 starts, Matt finished in the top-ten seven times.

The year 1998 would prove to be even better. In the team's first full Busch season, they finished in the top-five 17 times—good enough for second place in the final point standings. The championship was won by another young competitor named Dale Earnhardt Jr.

Matt trails rival Dale Earnhardt Jr. at Lowes Motor Speedway.

Matt put up another good year in 1999 recording 20 top-ten finishes. It was a great year for a young driver, but not quite good enough for the title. Matt came in third while his friend Dale Earnhardt Jr. posted his second consecutive championship season.

Near the end of the season, Matt and Robbie were invited to join Roush Racing, one of the biggest organizations in NASCAR. The partnership made the jump to NASCAR's Cup series much easier.

Although crashes are common, strict safety standards help reduce injuries.

ROOKIE OF THE YEAR

By the end of the 1999 season, Matt and his team were ready to race the Winston Cup series full time. Matt started 34 races in his 2000 **rookie** year. He won one race, the challenging Coca-Cola 600. More importantly, he finished in the top-ten 11 times.

In a close race for the Winston Cup Rookie of the Year award, Matt edged out a familiar rival, Dale Earnhardt Jr., who had also made the jump to the Cup series.

Matt Kenseth followed closely by Dale Earnhardt Jr.

FAST FACTS

NASCAR Point System for Each Race

Winner	driver earns 180 points
Runner-up	driver earns 170 points
3rd-6th position	points drop in 5-point increments (3rd position-165 points, 4th-160, 5th-155, and 6th-150 points)
7th-11th position	points drop in 4-point increments
12th-42nd position	points drop in 3-point increments
Last place	driver earns 34 points

Drivers can earn bonus points for leading a lap and leading the most laps

Crew Chief Robbie Reiser and Matt Kenseth watch a qualifying run at Pocono Raceway.

Matt Kenseth

As happy as Matt was about his Rookie of the Year honor, what he really wanted was a championship. In 2001, Matt raced in as many events as he could, looking for the edge he needed. He started only 23 Busch races, but still finished 18th in the standings. He also ran a full Winston Cup schedule and ended 13th in the point standings.

FAST FACTS

Robbie and Matt have maintained their close relationship over the years. Robbie is currently the crew chief for Matt's team. Robbie heads one of the fastest pit crews in NASCAR.

Matt continued to climb in the Cup rankings in 2002, finishing eighth, his best Winston season so far. He won five races and finished in the top-ten 19 times.

Matt celebrates after winning the 2003 Cup championship.

A CHAMPIONSHIP SEASON

Matt's determination paid off in 2003. In 36 starts, he won only a single Winston event, but he finished in the top-ten an amazing 25 times. He had more than enough points to win his first Winston Cup championship. In fact, he could have skipped the last race and still won the championship.

FAST FACTS

Matt was the last driver to win the Winston Cup championship. Nextel took over sponsorship of the top rated series beginning in 2004.

Matt sharing a moment with fans.

A CHAMPION DRIVER

Most champions seem to have one thing in common. They never seem to be satisfied with past victories. Matt has a Cup championship under his belt, but that hasn't slowed him down. Matt is back at it, working as hard as ever. He finished the 2004 season ranked eighth in the final point standings, and 2005 ranked sixth. Winning a second NASCAR Cup championship will not be easy, but if it were, Matt Kenseth probably would have chosen a different line of work.

Career Highlights

2005: Finished seventh in NASCAR's Nextel Cup series point standings
2004: Finished eighth in NASCAR Nextel Cup series point standings
2003: NASCAR Winston Cup series Champion
2002: Finished eighth in NASCAR Winston Cup series point standings
2001: Finished 13th in NASCAR Winston Cup series point standings
2000: NASCAR Winston Cup series Rookie of the Year
1999: Finished third in NASCAR Busch series point standing
1998: Finished second in NASCAR Busch series point standings

GLOSSARY

championship (CHAM pee uhn ship) — each driver is awarded points in a race, with winners earning the most. The driver with the most points at the end of a season wins the championship

NASCAR — National Association for Stock Car Auto Racing: the governing body for the Nextel Cup, Craftsman Truck, and Busch series, among others

rookie (ROOK ee) — a first-year driver

stock car (STOK KAR) — a commercially available car that has been modified for racing

INDEX

FURTHER READING

Burt, William. *NASCAR's Best: Stock Car Racing's Top Drivers.*
    Motorbooks International, 2004.
Cothren, Larry. *NASCAR's Next Generation.* Crestline, 2003.

WEBSITES TO VISIT

www.nascar.com
www.mattkenseth.com
www.roushracing.com

ABOUT THE AUTHORS

David and Patricia Armentrout have written many nonfiction books for young readers. They have had several books published for primary school reading. The Armentrouts live in Cincinnati, Ohio, with their two children.